THE KIDS'
MONEY
BOOK

Neale S. Godfrey

Illustrated by Justin Novak

CHECKERBOARD PRESS
NEW YORK

Contributing authors: John Couphas, Richard Wormser and Elizabeth Turner. Designed by R Studio T. Special thanks to Jane Lipp. The Children's Financial Network wishes to thank Peter Blank for his creative contributions in the development of the Greenstreets Common characters.

PHOTO CREDITS
Abbreviations: t = top, b = bottom, l = left, r = right, tl = top left, ml = middle left, bl = bottom left, etc.; ANS = The American Numismatic Society; SI = Smithsonian Institution, National Numismatic Collection Photo
Photo credits: 14–15 © SI; 17,20,22r © ANS; 22l (Photo by Else Sackler) Courtesy Department of Library Services, American Museum of Natural History; 25,26t © SI; 26b © ANS; 29 Courtesy of the Federal Reserve Bank of New York; 31,32–33 © ANS; 34,35t © SI; 35b,36 © ANS; 37 © SI; 38 Courtesy of Bureau of Engraving & Printing; 41,42 Official United States Mint Photograph; 43 Courtesy of Philadelphia Convention and Visitors Bureau; 45(ml,ll,tr) © SI; 45(all others) ANS; 52 Courtesy of New York Convention & Visitors Bureau; 53 Courtesy of the Federal Reserve Bank of New York; 54–55 Neg. No. K10931 Courtesy Department Library Services, American Museum of Natural History; 76–77,85t Courtesy American Express Travel Related Services Company; 85b Courtesy Visa USA; 86–87 © Design Photographers International, Inc.; 90 Courtesy National Park Service; 96 Courtesy of National Archives; 100–101 © New York Stock Exchange; 103 © Joel Gordon/Design Photographers International, Inc.; 106 © New York Stock Exchange

0 9 8 7 6 5 4 3 2

Dedication

To my two children Kyle and Rhett. I dedicate this book so they'll always know where they have spent their allowance.

Meet the People Who Live on Greenstreets Common:

Dollar Bill

"Buck," as his friends call him, is a very friendly dog. He wants to save and learn how to earn money, but sometimes his other friends take his mind off what he should be doing.

Penny Bright

She is a very clever cat. Penny knows her fashion and she knows her tax code; she is Today's Woman. Penny wants to be an entrepreneur when she grows up. She helps all of the kids in Greenstreets Common to save and spend wisely.

Not-So-Bright

He is Penny's brother. His motto of life is "All That Glitters Is Gold!" Not-So sometimes gets so enthusiastic that he diverts everyone's attention away from saving. Penny has to step in to "Save" the day.

Small Change

He is an energetic rabbit who is Dollar Bill's best friend. Most of the time he lives in Dollar Bill's pocket, because we always have "Small Change" in our pockets! He collects his money and counts it into his change maker. He's always there when Dollar Bill needs small change.

Common Cents

They are our friendly coins who teach the common sense approach to money. They'll give you money tips and valuable information to explain the best way to save and spend.

The Market Brothers: Bull & Bear

They run the Blue Chip Deli in Greenstreets Common. Bull likes to buy…buy…buy, and Bear likes to sell…sell…sell. They'll teach you how the stock market works. The stock market is like a large supermarket for stocks and bonds.

Opportunity

He teaches us to take advantage of unexpected occurrences in life. He may help us turn what seems to be a problem into an exciting chance to better ourselves. You never really see Opportunity because your opportunity is different from everyone else's. Yours is special, only you know what's in the box, because it's *your* opportunity. Remember, you never know when opportunity is going to knock!

Hedge

He's a hedgehog who sells balloons in Greenstreets Common. Hedge teaches us about the economy; in fact, he's a hedge against inflation. You'll see him floating with his balloons after he inflates them.

Automax

He is an automated teller machine (ATM). He teaches electronic banking. He is very ticklish, and when you push his buttons, he laughs.

Greenstreets Common

This is the fantasy village that our Greenstreets Common friends live in. They learn all about money in the village, how to use it, what it is, and how to save and spend wisely.

A NOTE TO PARENTS AND TEACHERS

"Children in the United States are financially illiterate." This statement comes from Paul Volcker, past chairman of the Federal Reserve, in response to the appalling results from a 1988 report from the Joint Council on Economic Education. It reflects the opinion of a great number of educators, economists, members of the financial community, government agencies, and most of all, parents. Children of all ages have only one clear understanding of money: HOW TO SPEND IT.

America has the lowest savings rate of any industrialized nation. Americans have more debt now than at any other time in history. The "American Dream," that children will live better than their parents, is fast becoming a nightmare. Many people are afraid of anything to do with money beyond paying their bills. They think of everything else as high finance, and much too complicated to deal with.

Saving, spending wisely, giving to people less fortunate, and planning for the future are topics that parents and educators rarely talk about with children. This failure to educate children about even the most fundamental financial facts of life is becoming an increasingly significant issue in light of our country's present economic problems.

Children, as well as adults, need to learn the uses and values of money along with the responsibility that comes with it; "Penny Wise, not Pound Foolish." This is a basic life skill.

Neale S. Godfrey, the founder and chairman of The Children's Financial Network, educates children about money in an entertaining way. She teaches that money itself is neither good nor bad. It is what is done with money that counts. THE KIDS' MONEY BOOK helps children and parents to discover how much fun understanding money can be, and how worthwhile the knowledge is!

CONTENTS

THE BEGINNING OF MONEY

WHAT IS MONEY?

WHAT WAS THE
SMALLEST MONEY
EVER USED?

WHAT DID PEOPLE
FIRST USE AS MONEY?

HOW DID MONEY
GET ITS NAME?

WHO WERE THE FIRST
PEOPLE TO USE
PAPER MONEY?

What is money?

Money is anything a group of people accept in exchange for goods or services. It is the coins and paper bills we use to pay someone for something we buy from them, or for a service they do for us.

What did people do before there was money?

Before people had money, they traded things they *had*—things they didn't need or had too much of—for things they *wanted*. People who lived near the sea traded fish for animal skins from hunters. Or they traded fish for wood from woodcutters. This kind of trading is called *bartering*. People got everything they needed by bartering.

Did people all over the world barter?

Yes. Neighbors bartered with each other. Different tribes and countries bartered, too. People also traveled from place to place to barter.

1. A **good**. Anything that you can trade with someone else.
2. A **service**. Any work that you can do for someone else.
3. To **barter**. To trade a good or a service with someone for a different good or service without using money.

Was bartering easy?

In the beginning it was, but it got complicated. If a man wanted a tent, but only had three camels, he had to find someone who was willing to exchange a tent for camels. Sometimes people traded for something they didn't want in the hope they could later trade it for something they did want.

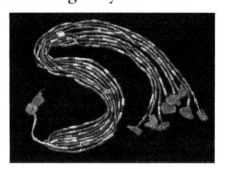

Wampum

FUN FACTS

In colonial times, when people wanted to come to America but didn't have the money to pay their boat fare, they would offer to work for seven years for anyone who would pay their way for them. These workers were called *indentured servants*.

Sometimes parents who wanted their daughter to marry a certain man would offer the man their daughter plus money or other valuable goods—like land or a cow—to improve the value of marrying their daughter. Sometimes it worked the other way around: A man had to give the woman's parents something valuable in order to be allowed to marry her. This still happens in some countries today.

Coastal Indians used shells as money. The shells were polished and strung together and called *wampum*. Early settlers, as well as the Indians, traded wampum for goods.

In 1626 Peter Minuit, a Dutch settler, traded with the local Indians $24 worth of beads for the Island of Manhattan. Today Manhattan is among the most valuable pieces of land in the world.

How did people decide how much of one thing to barter for another?

It wasn't very difficult when there were only a few things to barter. People soon got to agree on what could be traded for what. But when there were hundreds of items to swap, it got very complicated. For instance: Some people thought monkeys were worth more than coconuts, and some thought coconuts were worth more than monkeys. They had to decide how many of both they had to barter for a canoe. Some people thought canoes were worth one amount, and some thought they had a different value. Bartering got so complicated that people needed an easier way to trade.

Why did bartering stop?

Figuring out the value of things was tough. Plus, people had to carry everything they wanted to barter around with them—and that got very difficult. People needed to find a common measure of value to their possessions. This common measure is called a *medium of exchange*.

How do mediums of exchange work?

A medium of exchange is anything that a group of people agree has a certain value. If shells are the agreed upon medium of exchange, the value of everything is measured in shells, and everything is paid for in shells. If a hat costs five shells, a pair of shoes costs fifteen shells, and a coat, fifty. Whatever is bought is paid for in shells.

Buying and selling is a lot easier with an agreed upon medium of exchange. The coins and dollar bills we use today—or the shells, beads, or lumps of metal that were used thousands of years ago—are all examples of mediums of exchange.

For thousands of years the Chinese used cowrie shells as money. These smooth, beautiful shells of mollusks, found in the warm water of tropical oceans, were used by many people as a medium of exchange.

Mongolians used tea. Island dwellers used shells, and many people, including the Ethiopians, Chinese, and Romans, used salt as money.

Cowrie shells

Do people still barter today?

Yes. In some countries people still barter instead of using money, and even countries sometimes still barter with each other. Kids barter goods and services all the time. Exchanging baseball cards, stickers, or helping each other with chores —it's all bartering.

1. **Value**. The worth of something when measured in either goods, services, or a common medium of exchange.

2. **Bargaining**. A discussion about the value of an object for sale between the person who wants it and the person who wants to sell it.

What is the difference between things used as money and things used to barter?

Unlike corn or salt or beads, most money has no value except as a medium of exchange. Money is also different from other objects used to barter because it can be used by anyone in exchange for anything. For example, you could say that when you go to the store, you are bartering your quarter for a pack of gum, too. But you can use your quarter to buy anything else you want. The storekeeper can then also use the quarter for anything he wants. And the quarter has no other use except as a medium of exchange.

What did people first use as money?

Almost everything that was easy to carry around and easy to count was tried out. People used seeds, seashells, rocks, leather, animal furs, cows, sheep, salt, tea, tobacco, beads, fish hooks, dogs' teeth, feathers, the bristles from an elephant's tail, dead rats, and many, many other things. Some people even used human heads! Just about anything you can think of was probably tried as a medium of exchange.

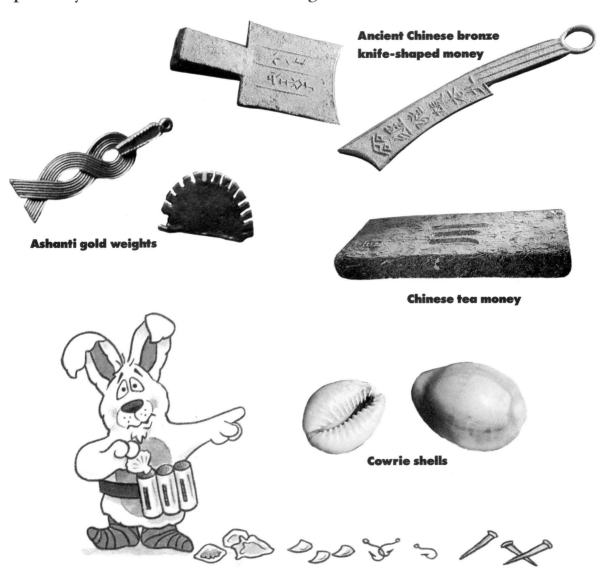

Ancient Chinese bronze knife-shaped money

Ashanti gold weights

Chinese tea money

Cowrie shells

Where was money first used?

No one knows for sure, but we know that about 5,000 years ago the people of Mesopotamia were using metal as money. But even before that, people had used other things for money.

Why was metal used for money?

Because most other mediums of exchange didn't work too well. Shells were okay, but seeds rotted or blew away in the wind, and cows were often hard to move. Many people agreed that the best mediums of exchange had to be small, easy to use, strong enough to last, and easily available. Metal money was the answer.

Who were the first people to use coins?

No one knows for sure. Some think it was the people of Mesopotamia 5,000 years ago. Others believe it was the people of Egypt, around 2500 B.C. But the first clearly recorded use of marked coins was by the Greeks just after 700 B.C.

What kinds of metals have been used to make money?

When people first decided that metal was the best material to use for money, they usually used the metals found locally. These metals varied from place to place.

Gold, silver, bronze, copper, and iron were the most common metals used, but lead and tin were also used. A natural mixture of gold and silver called *electrum* was used in Lydia around 600 B.C. Nuggets of electrum were found in rivers. Later coins made of gold and silver became the most valuable.

The first people to use these metals weighed pieces of gold and silver to decide how much they were worth. Some early metal money was shaped into specially designed pellets or trinkets that were given a certain value.

WORDS TO KNOW

1. To mint. To make coins out of metal.

2. A mint. A place where the coins of a country are made.

UNITED STATES MINT

SOME MINTS ARE NICE TO EAT!

24

When was money first minted?

By 700 B.C. each Greek city had its own distinct flat pieces of metal that were stamped with a picture or a design. These were the first true coins. By 500 B.C., coins were being used as money regularly in Greece and Rome.

Early Greek money

How did money get its name?

From the old Latin word *moneta*, which was the name given to the place in ancient Rome where money was first made and stored.

What is the lightest and the heaviest money ever used?

The lightest money ever was used on the Pacific island of Santa Cruz. This money was made of feathers. The heaviest money ever used was made of stone and used by the people of another Pacific island called Yap. These stones were twelve feet tall and weighed more than five hundred pounds.

Stone Yap money

What was the smallest money ever used?

Obelas, a type of money that was used in Greece, were smaller than an apple seed. People used to carry obelas in their mouth so that they wouldn't lose them, and hoped that they wouldn't sneeze or swallow!

Obelas and a penny

26

Four things that made metal money a best seller:

1. It was easy to carry—no matter where you went!

2. It didn't wear out easily.

3. There was a limited supply—it didn't grow on trees. But there was still enough so it wouldn't run out.

4. It could be changed when and if you wanted. One coin could have one value stamped on it and another coin another value. Old money could also be melted down to make new money.

Did money make trade with other countries easier?

Definitely. Money was a great help. Everything had an agreed upon value with money as the common medium of exchange. There were a few new complications because not all towns and countries used the same money. But it was much better than bartering.

Once money was invented, did everyone use it?

No. Because even though money made life easier, lots of people continued to barter, and people still barter today. At first, money was used only by wealthy people for important events like paying taxes, but for many day to day things people still bartered. Workers were often paid for their services with food, clothing, or a place to live.

WORDS TO KNOW

1. **Counterfeit**. To make a copy of something that people will think is real.
2. **Currency**. Any kind of money that is used as a medium of exchange.
3. **Denomination**. The name of a group of things.

Where was gold first used as money?

A country called Lydia, which is now part of Turkey, was the first country to use gold as money. The king Croesus, who lived around 600 B.C., was so wealthy that even today people sometimes describe a rich person by saying, "He is as rich as Croesus."

FUN FACTS

Pure gold is called 24 carat gold. 14 carat gold is 14 parts pure gold and 10 parts of a mixture of silver and copper. 18 carat gold is made up of 18 parts gold and 6 parts silver and copper.

Gold ingots

How is the weight of gold measured?

Gold is weighed in pennyweights. Twenty pennyweights is equal to one ounce, Troy weight. One Troy ounce is equal to 1.0971 Avoirdupois ounces—which are the sort of ounces we use every day to weigh things.

How much gold is there in the world?

It's not known exactly how much gold there is, as new deposits could still be found. But all the gold that has ever been mined in the world weighs about 95,000 tons. It could be made into a cube measuring 19 yards on each side. As far as we know, virtually none of the mined gold has been lost.

What color is gold?

In its pure form real gold is a golden color. But pure gold is very soft, so gold is usually mixed with small amounts of other metals to make it harder. Sometimes this changes its color. Mixing gold with silver or copper is very common. But by mixing gold with platinum or silver, gold turns a silvery color. It looks reddish when mixed with copper and green when mixed with iron. One of the rarest forms is black gold, which is gold that contains a mineral called bismuth.

FUN FACTS

In Greek mythology King Midas wished that everything he touched would turn to gold. His wish was granted, but eventually he asked that his wish be canceled—because even the food he touched turned to gold! Today when someone is very successful at making a lot of money, we say he or she has "the Midas touch."

What was the idea behind paper money?

Coins are fairly easy to carry around, but if you have a lot of them, they can be heavy! Paper money is much lighter to carry. It is also a lot cheaper to make than coins.

Who were the first people to use paper money?

No one knows for sure, but the earliest known paper money was made by the Chinese and dates from around A.D.1300.

Chinese paper money

TRAL BAN
OF ALABAMA
One Hundred Dollars
Montgomery

Cash.

WHERE WAS THE
FIRST U.S. MINT?

WHY DO SOME COINS
HAVE RIDGES
AROUND THE EDGES?

MONEY IN THE
UNITED STATES

WHAT DO ALL THE
DESIGNS ON A DOLLAR
BILL MEAN?

HOW CAN YOU GET
NEW MONEY FOR OLD?

WHY IS THERE A
TINY LETTER ON THE
FACE OF A QUARTER?

What money was used in Colonial America?

Coins from Spain, England, France, and Holland were used.

How was small change made in colonial times?

The Spanish dollar was often cut into eight pieces called "bits." A quarter of a dollar coin was called "two bits." Today, some people still call a quarter "two bits."

Pieces of eight

When was the first paper money issued in America?

In 1690 the Massachusetts Bay Colony established a bank and issued paper money. It was in denominations ranging from two shillings to five pounds, and was used to pay soldiers.

During the American War of Independence the Continental Congress (the American government) issued paper money. These paper notes were called *continentals*. Prices rose so rapidly and so many were printed that they became worthless. By the end of the war, a whole barrel of continentals couldn't buy a piece of cheese.

A Continental note

FUN FACTS

At one time the Treasury Department authorized a variety of different bills for special occasions. One of the most beautiful series commemorated the Educational Bill of 1880, and was printed to honor education.

Educational Bill

When did the United States begin using dollars?

In 1792 the United States adopted the dollar as its unit of money. Until then many different kinds of money were used.

Where was the first U.S. mint?

The first United States mint was established in Philadelphia in 1792.

When were the first U.S. coins minted?

In 1794 silver coins were minted and in 1795 gold coins were minted. The first cents and half-cents were minted in 1793.

Early gold coins

FUN FACTS

A dime gets its name from *dismes*, a system based on ten. The Latin word for *ten* is *dismes*. A quarter gets its name because it is a quarter—or one-fourth—of a dollar.

A dollar gets its name from the German word *Taler*, which is shortened from the word *Joachimsthaler*, a coin made in the town of Joachimsthal in Czechoslovakia.

What were the first gold American coins?

There were three different gold coins, each worth a different amount. The eagle was worth ten dollars, the half-eagle was worth five dollars, and the quarter eagle was worth $2.50. Gold coins continued to be used until 1934.

Early gold coins

What money was used after America became independent?

An act of Congress in 1793 made foreign coins in circulation acceptable as American money. But many people were reluctant to use foreign coins because there wasn't an exact value to each coin. One coin that was acceptable was the Spanish dollar, sometimes called "pieces of eight."

When were the first United States national bank notes issued?

Until the mid-1800s banks printed money. These bank notes promised that the bank would exchange the note for gold or silver. But sometimes the banks didn't have enough gold or silver to keep their promise. The government decided to stop this. So in 1861 the government printed the first United States paper money. These notes were called *greenbacks* because the back of the bills were green. This currency was created by the Treasury Department, a new part of the government designed to control money. After 1864 the government allowed banks to print paper money as long as they kept some of the bank's savings with the government. But this led to confusion. Banks in different states, and even banks in the same town, issued different types of money. Sometimes banks issued bills worth only 3 cents; sometimes the bills were worth a lot more. By 1863 there were thousands of bills in existence, all from different banks—and many of these were counterfeit. Since 1877 all paper money in the United States has been issued by the Treasury Department.

The Bureau of Engraving and Printing in Washington, D. C.

Where is money minted and printed today?

Today all the coins we use are produced in one of four government mints. All the bills we use are printed at the U.S. Bureau of Engraving and Printing in Washington, D.C.

What are coins made of today?

Pennies are made of copper-coated zinc alloy. Nickels are a mixture of copper and nickel. Dimes, quarters, half dollars, and dollars have a copper core covered with an alloy of copper and nickel. Although gold and silver were used in coins for many years, the government stopped using gold in 1934.

WORDS TO KNOW

1. **Molten.** Melted metal.

2. **Annealing.** Heating a material to make it softer and less brittle so that it can be worked.

3. **Cladding.** Metal bonded to an inner core of another metal.

4. **Ingot.** Metal cast in a convenient shape before it is made into something else.

Why do some coins have ridges around the edges?

Early gold and silver coins were smooth around the edges. But some people shaved the edges of the coins and later sold the valuable scraps. Ridges were put on the edges of the coins so that people could not cheat in this way. Even though quarters and dimes are no longer made of silver, they still have ridges around the edges today.

Is there a special name for coins with the ridges?

Coins with ridges are called *milled coins.*

When were the coins we use today first introduced?

All the coins we use today were introduced beginning in 1900.

Whose images are on these coins?

1. Penny?
2. Nickel?
3. Dime?
4. Quarter?
5. Half dollar?

1. Abraham Lincoln 2. Thomas Jefferson 3. Franklin D. Roosevelt
4. George Washington 5. John F. Kennedy

Why is there a tiny letter on the face of a quarter?

This tiny letter to the right of the face is called the mint mark and tells you where the coin was minted. There are four mints that make coins in the United States. Each has its own code. *D* is for Denver, Colorado; *O* is for New Orleans, Louisiana; *P* is for Philadelphia, Pennsylvania; and *S* is for San Francisco, California.

FUN FACTS

At one time or another in the United States there has been a twenty-cent coin, a half-cent coin, a two-cent coin, and even a three-cent coin.

The Lincoln penny that we still use today was first issued in 1909 to mark the 100th anniversary of President Abraham Lincoln's birth.

How coins are made:

Pure metals are weighed and melted together to make the alloys needed for the coins. While still molten, the alloys are cast into ingots. Machines roll the ingots out into sheets. Dimes, quarters, and dollars are made from three sheets of metal bonded together in a process called cladding. Blanks the same diameter as the coins are punched from the sheets. Penny and nickel blanks are sent to the "annealing" room where they are softened slightly, cleaned, and polished. They are then put through an edge rolling machine which produces a raised rim. Finally the designs on both sides of the coin are stamped on at the same time. The edges of dimes, quarters, and dollars are milled in this final stamping process.

Coin blanks are punched out of the metal sheets, like cookies from a sheet of dough.

The completed coins are loaded into machines that automatically count them and drop them into bags. The sealed bags are then weighed on scales that are so sensitive that even if one coin is the wrong weight, the machine records it. The coins are then put into circulation via banks.

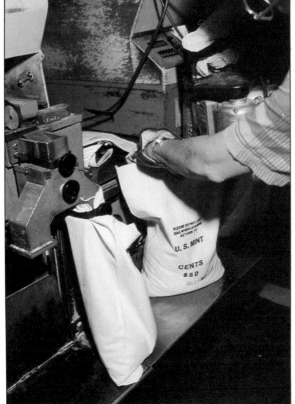

Coin-counting machine

FUN FACTS

By law, the design of any coin must be kept for at least twenty-five years.

42

How were coins made in early times?

The Ancient Romans made their bronze coins by pouring molten metal into molds. This method, called casting, was also used by the Chinese and Japanese. However, most coins made before the invention of the coining press were struck one by one using a special hammer.

FUN FACTS

Nickels are made of 75% copper and 25% nickel. Pennies are made of bronze which is 95% copper and 5% zinc.

The outside of dimes, quarters, and dollars are 75% copper and 25% nickel. Their cores are pure copper.

United States Mint, Philadelphia

How much silver is there in a dime?

Since 1965 there has been no silver at all in our dimes and quarters. This was because there was a world shortage of silver and it was necessary to conserve silver supplies for industry and military use. Since 1970 our dollars have not been made of silver either.

What was the difference between the value of gold and silver coins and paper money?

Gold and silver coins were worth the exact value of gold or silver that they were made from. The coins could be exchanged for goods for the value of the gold or silver. Paper money was different. The paper itself was worth nothing. It was a promise from the bank to pay the holder of the note the value that was printed on the money.

When did the bills we use today first come into circulation?

In 1913 the government stopped letting private banks print their own notes. The government bought all existing notes from the banks and a new system was started. The government bank began issuing all the notes. This was the beginning of the bills we use today, but these bills were bigger than our modern ones. In 1929 the Federal Reserve redesigned the notes and made them smaller, and they have remained the same size ever since.

Early American paper money

Whose images are on the following U.S. bills?

One? Two? Five? Ten? Twenty? Fifty? Hundred?

Which of these men was not a president?

Alexander Hamilton and Benjamin Franklin. Hamilton was secretary of the Treasury in George Washington's government, and Benjamin Franklin was one of the founders of the United States who helped to write the Constitution.

What kind of ink is used to print our money?

A special ink made from a secret formula. If you rub the surface of the green side of a bill with a tissue, you will see that some of the ink has rubbed off. This is because the ink never completely dries.

What kind of paper is paper money made of?

The paper used to make money is a special blend of linen and cotton. It is illegal for anyone to make this kind of paper without special permission from the Bureau of Engraving and Printing.

What is the largest denomination of a bill ever printed in America?

The $100,000 bill. It was used only to make payments between banks. For a while the Bureau of Engraving and Printing was making $500, $1,000, $5,000, and $10,000 bills, but since no one used them, they are no longer made. Today the largest bill in circulation is the $100 bill.

FUN FACTS

It's the law! Federal law states that any picture of American money cannot be printed its actual size. It must be printed either bigger or smaller than it really is. No matter what size the picture is, the bills cannot be reproduced in color. Which is why this one is black and white!

What do the designs on a dollar bill mean?

This mark tells you which Federal Reserve Bank first issued the bill. Although all the bills are printed at the U.S. Bureau of Engraving and Printing in Washington, D.C., they are issued from different Federal Reserve Banks across the country.

Federal Reserve Banks and the codes that indicate their districts:

Boston A
New York B
Philadelphia C
Cleveland D
Richmond E
Atlanta F

Chicago G
St. Louis H
Minneapolis I
Kansas City J
Dallas K
San Francisco L

This is the serial number of the bill. Every single bill of the same denomination made in the United States has a different number. Counterfeiters are often caught when they make a lot of bills with the same serial number.

This is the signature of the treasurer of the United States at the time the bill is printed.

This is the great seal of the United States. The unfinished pyramid symbolizes growth. The eye represents the watchful gaze of God.

This number is the series identification number. It shows the date that this bill design was first used. A new design may only mean that the name of the treasurer has changed.

The eagle symbolizes the thirteen original colonies of America. There are thirteen stars above the eagle's head, thirteen arrows in one claw, and an olive branch with thirteen leaves and thirteen olives held in the other claw.

FUN FACTS

Money Expressions

Money expressions are part of our language. Our coins and bills have become words and phrases. The following are all expressions we use. Have you heard of any of these?

"Penny pincher"—a frugal person

"Red cent"—your last penny

"Two cents' worth"—some opinion a person feels he always must give

"A penny for your thoughts"—what you say when you want to know what someone is thinking

"A plugged nickel"—something worthless

"Nickel and diming"—being cheap

"Dime a dozen"—a cheap deal

"Put cash on the barrelhead"—paying cash now

"Your bottom dollar"—the lowest price

"You look like a million bucks!"—You look terrific!

50

What happens to paper money when it wears out?

Every day at every bank, worn and damaged paper money is removed from circulation and returned to a Federal Reserve Bank. The bills are shredded and most of the pieces burned. The average life of a one dollar bill is about seventeen to eighteen months. New paper money is made only to replace the bills that are worn out. There is strict control over the amount of money that is printed. Every year tens of millions of dollars' worth of worn-out bills are destroyed.

How can you get new money for your old?

If you give a partially destroyed or torn bill to the Treasury, they will replace it with a whole new one. If you have at least a little more than half the bill you can have it replaced. Every day the U.S. Treasury receives thousands of dollars that have been badly mangled or destroyed.

FUN FACTS

The U.S. Treasury has received and replaced money that has been stuffed in mattresses and forgotten. It has received money that has been burned, chewed by cows, and even some money that was hidden in a shotgun and forgotten until the owner fired the gun and the money was blown out!

How much money is there in circulation in the U.S.A. today?

Approximately 215 billion dollars in coins and bills. That's $215,000,000,000. That much money in one dollar bills would fill up the two World Trade Center buildings in New York City!

World Trade Center In New York

Where is the largest single deposit of federal gold in the U.S.A.?

In the Federal Reserve Bank of New York. The gold is worth 140 billion dollars! Most of it is owned by foreign countries. The gold is locked in a vault that is buried eighty feet underground and is half the size of a football field. The gold is shaped into bars—each bar is about the size of a skinny brick. Most of America's gold is in Kentucky in a place called Fort Knox.

Is Fort Knox part of the Federal Reserve?

No. Although Fort Knox is where the United States stores most of its gold, Fort Knox is an army base in Kentucky.

Gold stored in the Federal Reserve Bank of New York

Why does the government store gold in Fort Knox?

The gold in Fort Knox belongs to the U.S. Government. Originally the government stored gold because U.S. dollars were backed by gold. That meant that you could bring paper money to a bank and exchange it for the equivalent amount of gold. This is no longer true, but the government continues to guard the gold it has because it is so valuable.

WHEN DID BANKING
BEGIN?

HOW DO BANKS
EARN MONEY?

ALL ABOUT
BANKING

HOW DO I KNOW
MY MONEY IS
SAFE IN A BANK?

HOW IS A CHECK READ
ELECTRONICALLY?

WHAT HAPPENS IF I
WRITE A CHECK WHEN
I HAVE NO MONEY?

What is a bank?

A bank is a safe place to keep money. But a bank is also a business that performs a number of services for its customers and needs to make a profit. Banks use customers' deposits of money to lend to other people who need money. There are rules to make sure that the bank doesn't lend out too much money so that when a customer wants his or her money it should be there for them. The bank pays for the use of the money, and the bank charges people who borrow money a fee. The fee the bank charges people who borrow money is called *interest*. There are banks all over the country and all over the world.

Are there special rules banks must obey?

There are many. Here are some important ones:

1. Banks must insure their customers' deposits.

2. Banks must keep a percentage of their deposits in a Federal Reserve Bank.

3. Banks must tell customers the interest rate on a loan, and how much total interest they will have to pay on a loan.

4. All agreements that bank customers sign must be written in plain English so that the customer understands exactly what it is he or she is signing.

5. Banks may not discriminate against anyone on account of age, sex, religion, race, or ethnic group.

6. Banks may not make loans unless they are sure they will be repaid.

Are all banks the same?

No. There are different kinds of banks in America.

1. Commercial banks. This type of bank deals with people and businesses. They offer services like checking and savings accounts and loans. Commercial banks are owned by their stockholders and the profits go to them, if the bank pays dividends.

2. Thrift banks, savings and loans, and credit unions are very similar. These mostly provide mortgages so people can buy homes. Most savings and loans, credit unions, and thrifts used to be owned by the depositors and the profits were shared among them. But banking is changing, and commercial banks, savings and loans, and thrifts are becoming more alike.

3. Investment banks are not really banks. They are firms that give investment advice. They also buy and sell stocks and bonds from companies and government agencies and sell smaller quantities of them to investors and individuals at a profit. Investment banks may not accept deposits or make loans.

4. The Central Bank of the United States is called the Federal Reserve System. The Federal Reserve System includes the 12 regional banks.

When did banking begin?

Banking began thousands of years ago. In ancient times some temples were used to store precious metals, exchange foreign coins, or make loans. People were afraid to steal from a holy temple for fear of making the gods angry. As early as 2000 years ago, in Babylon, a record was kept of how much precious metal each person deposited in the temple.

In ancient Greece, where each city had its own coins, money changers exchanged the coins from one city for those from another, and exchanged coins for gold or silver. They charged a fee for doing this. These services encouraged trade between different cities and foreign countries. Later in history goldsmiths acted as bankers by keeping valuable possessions for people in their vaults.

FUN FACTS

About A.D. 1100, what we call banking today—selling, borrowing, and trading—started in Italy. Early Italian bankers conducted their business on a street bench. *Banca* is the Italian word for "bench," and that is where we get the word *bank*.

BANKING

1. **Check**. A written order to a bank to pay a specified amount of money to a specified person or company, from money on deposit with the bank.

2. **Loan**. An amount of money that is lent for a certain period of time. Usually, an agreement is made stating how long the loan is for and how much interest the borrower will pay the lender.

3. **Savings**. Money that is saved somewhere so that it can be used later.

4. **Mortgage money**. Money loaned by a bank for the purpose of buying a house or other property. It is secured by the property. That means that if the money is not repaid, the bank can take the property.

5. **Fee**. A charge fixed by an institution. Any fixed charge.

6. **Interest.** The amount of money charged by a bank for lending money, or paid on money left in an interest bearing account.

Where did piggy banks get their names?

From a kind of clay called *pygg*. Money stored at home in a jar made of this clay came to be called pygg banks. Eventually the name changed to piggy bank, and people actually began making them in the shape of pigs.

How do I know my money is safe in a bank?

Banks do not keep a great deal of money in the bank building. The money that the banks do keep is stored in fireproof vaults. And in most banks the money is insured against fire, theft, or bank failure by the FDIC (the Federal Deposit Insurance Corporation). Before you deposit money in a bank account, make sure the bank is insured.

How do banks earn money?

Banks, like any business, must make a profit. They do this mostly by making loans and investments. Banks charge a higher interest on money they lend than on money they borrow from their customers.

What happened when banks made loans without good security?

When banks made loans that were not repaid, they often didn't have enough money to honor their bank notes. Many banks went bankrupt and their customers lost their money.

Can banks lend or invest all the money that is deposited with them?

No. The Federal Reserve requires banks to keep a certain percentage of the money deposited in the bank on reserve, so that when people want their money it's there. Most of the money that a bank has exists only as a computer entry. Banks lend out more money than they actually have. They know from experience that not everybody is going to want all their money on the same day. So they lend out the money people have deposited with them to other customers who want to borrow it.

What is a savings account?

A bank account where a bank or savings institution keeps money for you so you can use it at a later date. As long as the money stays in the savings account, the bank pays you interest. There are several different kinds of savings accounts—each pays a different amount of interest.

1. A Passbook Account. Every time you make a deposit or a withdrawal you must present your passbook to the bank for the transaction to be entered. You may also mail your deposit to the bank, but you must send your book along with the deposit.

2. A CD—a Certificate of Deposit—is money you deposit for an agreed amount of time. Because the bank knows how long you will leave your money, it can lend it and not worry about when you will need it. Therefore the bank will pay you a slightly higher amount of interest. If you withdraw your money early, you must pay a penalty.

3. A Money Market Account is similar to a checking account, but it earns interest. Usually you can only write a limited number of checks each month, so the bank pays you a little less interest, because you can draw money when you want.

4. An IRA (Individual Retirement Account) is a savings account for your retirement. The government allows you to delay paying taxes on the part of your wages that you save in an IRA.

5. A Keogh Account is like an IRA, but it is for people who are self-employed.

Why do banks pay you for looking after your money instead of you paying them?

Because by putting your money into the bank, you are really letting the bank use your money for a while. The bank can lend your money to someone who wants to borrow it. The person has to pay the bank interest. But he or she pays the bank more interest than the bank pays you. So the bank earns money by being the in-between person. Just like a money changer in the old days.

Is interest from loans the only way a bank can earn money?

No. Banks also earn money by charging customers for other services besides loans, and by investing their own money in other banks, in government bonds, and in other investments.

Must a bank agree to open an account for anyone who applies?

Banks are not required to open accounts for everyone who applies. They may require identification, and verification of the person's identity and job. They may have any restrictions they want, as long as they are not based on race, sex, age, or religion.

Why have a bank account?

A bank account is a safe place to keep your money until you need it. Most people have two bank accounts: a checking account and a savings account.

What is a checking account?

A checking account is one that lets you keep your money in a safe place and still use it anytime you need it. Instead of having to carry cash to pay for everything you buy, you can write a check. When you open a checking account, you get checks from your bank. A check tells your bank how much you want them to pay from your bank account into someone else's bank account. All checks say: *"Pay to the order of."* You must always have enough money in your checking account when you write a check. Paying by check gives you proof that you have paid a bill. Another name for a checking account is a *demand deposit* account because you can get your money from the bank when you ask for it by writing a check.

WHAT ARE YOU DOING?

I'M KITING A CHECK!

How to write a check.

Always write your check in ink so that the information cannot be erased or changed.

1. The date you are writing the check.

2. The name of the person or company you want to pay.

3. The amount in numbers

4. Your signature. It must match your signature card at the bank.

5. The dollar in words and the cents in numbers as shown. Always draw a line to fill the whole space. This prevents anyone from adding anything to your amount.

DOLLAR BILL
GREEN STREETS COMMON
USA

0001

June 5 19 91
TODAY'S DATE

PAY TO THE ORDER OF _Nickel Angelo Gallery_ $ | 25.50 |
WHO GETS THE MONEY?   HOW MUCH MONEY, IN NUMBERS?

Twenty-five and 50/100 _____ DOLLARS
HOW MUCH MONEY, IN WORDS?

Penny Bright
SIGN YOUR NAME HERE

Children's Financial Network inc.

1:21485020383

NOT NEGOTIABLE

What happens to a check after it's written?

We know that money doesn't have to be green, silver, or gold to be worth something. Today most money is never seen or even touched—it is transferred from bank to bank electronically. Computers speed the way banks do business. It's a lot faster for a computer to transfer money than to carry millions of pieces of paper money and coins from one bank to another. Especially when some of the banks are halfway around the world.

The life of a check.

1. Penny Bright in Greenstreets Common buys a picture from an art dealer in San Francisco. She mails a check to pay for it.

7. Now the clearing bank which serves Greenstreets Common pays the San Francisco clearing bank.

6. Greenstreets Common Bank then tells its clearing bank to subtract the amount from its account.

66

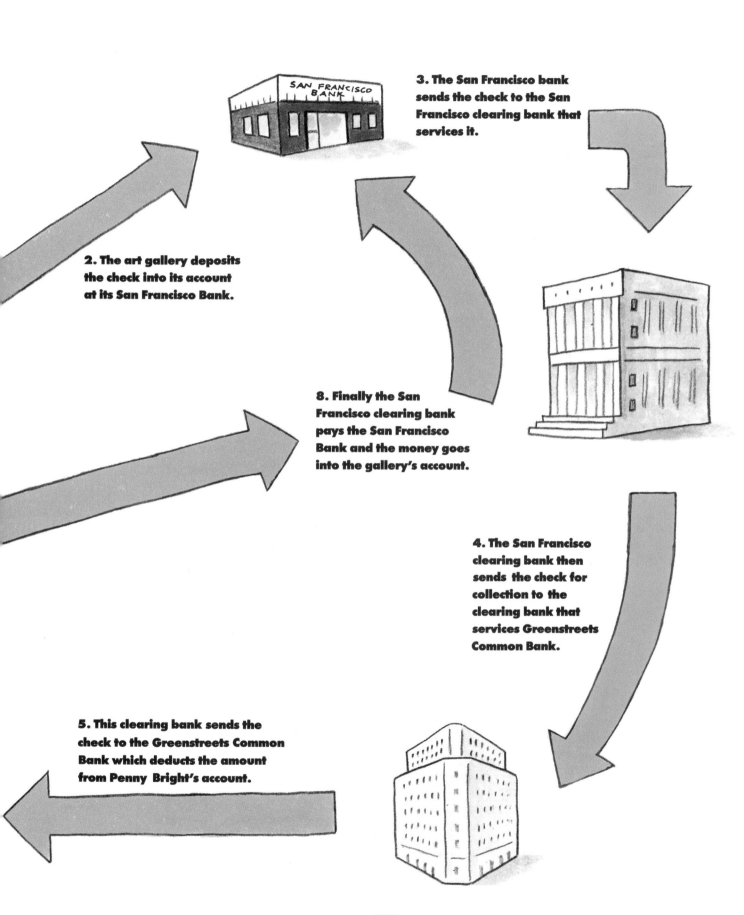

3. The San Francisco bank sends the check to the San Francisco clearing bank that services it.

2. The art gallery deposits the check into its account at its San Francisco Bank.

8. Finally the San Francisco clearing bank pays the San Francisco Bank and the money goes into the gallery's account.

4. The San Francisco clearing bank then sends the check for collection to the clearing bank that services Greenstreets Common Bank.

5. This clearing bank sends the check to the Greenstreets Common Bank which deducts the amount from Penny Bright's account.

SAN FRANCISCO BANK

67

How is a check read electronically?

Check processing is done automatically by high-speed electronic machines that "read" the sorting instructions printed in magnetic ink along the bottom of the check. About 100,000 checks can be sorted in an hour.

The routing number is repeated in a different format in the upper right-hand corner of the check. This number is used in manual processing.

The check number.

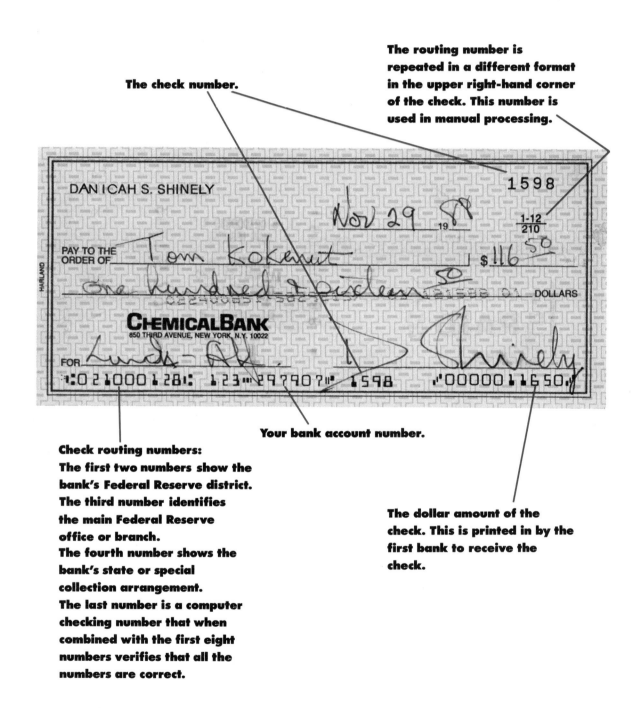

Check routing numbers:
The first two numbers show the bank's Federal Reserve district.
The third number identifies the main Federal Reserve office or branch.
The fourth number shows the bank's state or special collection arrangement.
The last number is a computer checking number that when combined with the first eight numbers verifies that all the numbers are correct.

Your bank account number.

The dollar amount of the check. This is printed in by the first bank to receive the check.

The depositor's endorsement. All checks must be endorsed or stamped by the depositor before they are deposited.

The bank where the check was processed.

The process date.

The payment stamp indicates that your bank has certified that you have enough money in the bank to pay this check and it has been paid.

If I keep writing checks, how do I know how much money I have in my bank account?

Every time you write a check you must keep a record of the check. Some checks have a part just for this called *check stubs*. Other checkbooks have a separate section called a *register* where you write down the information. Other checks are made to create a carbon copy of each check you write. By keeping track of how much money you have spent with checks, you will always know how much money you have in the bank.

What is a bank statement?

At the end of the month the bank sends a statement to each customer. It tells them how much money they have spent that month, and how much they still have in the bank.

How do you "balance" a checkbook?

Balancing a checkbook means making sure that what your statement says you have spent or deposited is the same amount that your own records show. This is very simple to do. Just follow these steps:

1. Write down the closing balance which the bank has listed.

2. Add to this amount any deposits you made which the bank has not listed. Don't forget the ones you may have made since the statement was issued.

3. Subtract from this new total the amounts of any checks written or withdrawals made which did not appear on your bank statement.

4. Compare the end figure with the balance in your own records. The two numbers should be the same, and this is the amount of money you actually have in your checking account.

What happens if I accidentally write a check for more money than I have in the bank?

It is illegal to write a check if you don't have enough money in the bank to cover your check. But if it is an accident the check "bounces"—which means the money is not paid and the unpaid check is returned to the person or company you gave the check to. You will also be asked to give the company cash or another check. If you give them a check, you have to remember that it will "bounce" again if you don't put more money in the bank first. Usually your bank will charge you a fee for writing a "bad" check. And often the person or company that you gave the "bad" check to will charge you a fee as well.

What happens if I write a check when I know I haven't enough money in the bank to pay the check?

It is a crime to write a check if you don't have enough money in the bank to cover the check. If you "bounce" a check and then don't pay the person you gave the "bad" check to with cash or a new check, you can be sent to jail.

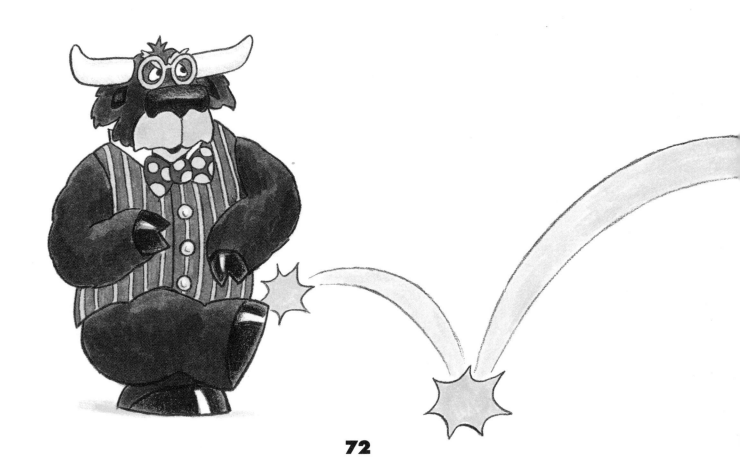

Why are checking accounts important?

Checks have become the most common medium of exchange in America and throughout most of the world. People write checks more often than they use cash. In many ways, checks have replaced paper money and coins. Today there are approximately 125 million checking accounts in America, and new ones are being opened every day.

Is it better to use checks than cash?

Checks aren't necessarily better, but in many ways they are easier. You can send checks through the mail to pay bills, instead of having to carry the exact amount of cash to pay the companies you owe money to. Checks are also safer to carry than money because a blank check has no value. A check that has been cleared by a bank is proof that a bill has been paid.

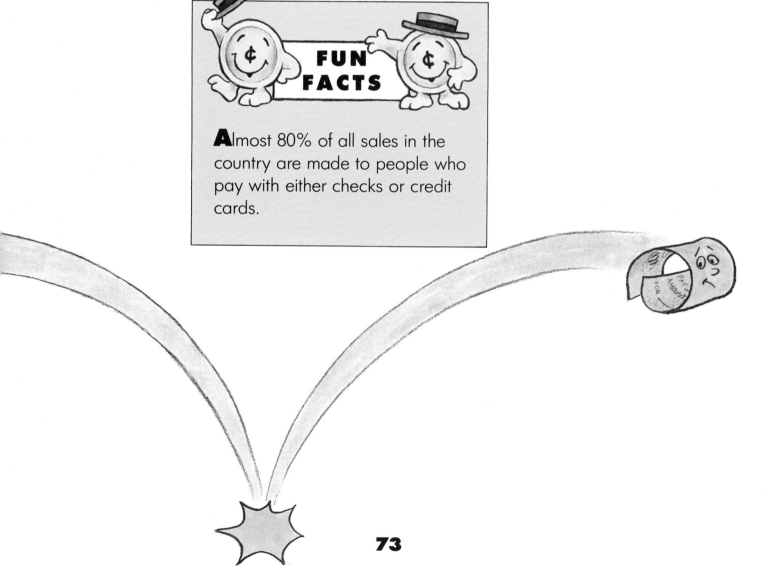

FUN FACTS

Almost 80% of all sales in the country are made to people who pay with either checks or credit cards.

What is a safe way to send money through the mail if I don't have a bank account?

You can buy a money order from a post office or a bank. It is just like a check, but you don't need a bank account to buy one. It can be cashed anywhere in the country. A money order states whom you want the money to be paid to. The person cashing the money order must show identification when he or she cashes it.

What is a traveler's check?

People who take trips to different places can use traveler's checks instead of carrying large amounts of money that might get lost or stolen. They are a safe way to carry money to places that won't take a credit card or a personal check. You can buy traveler's checks at banks, and if you wish you may buy the checks in a foreign currency. Usually the bank charges 1% for the checks.

What is a bank card?

A bank card is a small plastic card that lets you use your bank's Automated Teller Machine (ATM)—also called a *cash machine*. The ATM card has a secret number (PIN number) encoded electronically on it. With an ATM card, you use your bank whenever you want to, day or night. You can deposit money, transfer money, withdraw money, and even pay some bills. You can do nearly all your banking electronically from an ATM machine.

What is a googol?

A googol is a 1 followed by a hundred zeros. A mathematician, who needed a name for this number, got the word from his baby, who said the word *googol* while learning to talk. It is written: 10,000,000,000,000,000,000, 000,000,000,000,000,000,000,000,000,000,000,000,000,000,000, 000,000,000,000,000,000,000,000,000,000—that's a googol!

WHAT IS CREDIT?

WHAT IS A LINE OF CREDIT?

WHAT SHOULD I DO BEFORE I BORROW MONEY?

HOW DO PEOPLE GET CREDIT?

WHAT IS A CREDIT CHECK?

HOW DO BANKS EARN MONEY FROM CREDIT CARDS?

What is credit?

Credit comes from the Latin word *creditus*, meaning "to trust." When someone lends you money, he or she is trusting you to repay it.

Credit is not a right—it is a privilege. You earn the right to have credit. You must show you are responsible to get credit. Credit means that someone will lend you money and give you time to pay it back, usually for a fee. Credit enables you to buy now and pay later. When a bank lends you money, it is giving you credit. Consumers use credit to buy the things they need: houses, clothes, cars, television sets, and also if they have financial emergencies. Businesses use credit to expand and grow; governments use credit to build roads or bridges or to run their town, city, state, or country.

Who offers credit?

Banks, businesses, and individuals give credit. A store that gives credit allows you to buy now and pay later. A repairperson who mends something and then sends you a bill is giving you credit. He or she trusts you to pay the bill. A local grocery store may give a good customer credit by letting him or her buy things and pay for them later.

How do banks give credit?

Banks give credit through installment loans, lines of credit, mortgages, and credit cards. Before a bank will give credit it will run a credit check to make sure that the person pays his or her debts.

Will a bank give credit to anyone who asks for it?

No. A bank will only give credit to someone it feels sure will pay back the loan. Very often if you have never had a loan from a bank before, you will need collateral or have to have someone cosign the loan—such as a parent who has a good credit history.

Are there other types of credit?

Department stores offer a form of credit called *installment credit*. For example, if you buy a television set for $240 and the store allows you to take twelve months to pay for it, you agree to pay $20, plus interest, every month for twelve months.

What is the prime rate?

The prime rate is the interest rate that banks charge their best (biggest) customers.

What is interest?

Banks earn money by charging a fee when they make a loan. This charge is called interest. It can be compared with the profit shopkeepers charge for things they sell in their shops. If a shopkeeper adds 40% onto any item and then resells it, something that costs him $1.00 will be sold at $1.40. Banks work on the same principle, but on much smaller percentages. Interest can also be considered a fee you pay the bank for "renting" money to you. A bank might charge you an 8% fee or interest. For instance, if you borrow $1,200 at 8% interest and pay it back over three years:

Amount owed	Principal	Repayment of Principal	Interest
1st year	$1,200	$ 400	$ 96
2nd year	800	400	64
3rd year	400	400	32
		$1,200	$192

Therefore you actually pay the bank $1,392.00 for "renting" $1,200 to you over three years.

What is a line of credit?

A line of credit means that an agreed amount of money is waiting for you in the bank whenever you want it. Any money you borrow against your line of credit, you must repay, plus interest. But if you don't use any money from your line of credit, you pay nothing. If you have a $5,000 line of credit, and you only use $1,000, then you will only have to pay back $1,000 plus interest.

A line of credit differs from an installment loan in that the installment loan gives you all the money you want at one time, and you pay a fixed amount back each month.

What should I do before I borrow money?

The first rule before you make a major purchase is to "shop around." That way you can be sure you get the best price. When you borrow money from a bank or sign up for a credit card the same rule applies. Shop around. Check out what different banks charge. Some banks charge the customer for applying for a loan, others don't. Some banks offer lower interest rates, but charge a fee if you pay your loan late. Different banks offer different interest rates. Also, there is always a trade-off between the amount of time you take to pay back a loan, and the amount of money you can afford to pay each month. If you can only afford a small monthly payment it will take you longer to pay back the loan. The longer you take to repay a loan, the more interest you will have to pay to the bank.

What is a credit card?

A credit card lets people buy goods or services at places that accept the card, and pay later. Unless you pay the full amount owed on your credit card each month, the goods or services you buy with a credit card are more expensive than those you pay for at the time you purchase them. This is because the interest you pay each month is added to the cost of your purchase. A credit card is not a license to spend money and it should be used very carefully. It is very important not to accumulate debt that you can't pay.

Many stores and companies issue credit cards that can only be used at their establishments. But banks and other financial institutions issue cards that can be used at any place that accepts them.

How does the bank earn money from credit cards?

Most banks charge you an annual fee for the use of the credit card. Every month the bank sends cardholders a bill showing everything they bought (charged) with the card that month. Some banks allow cardholders to pay just part of the bill. If a cardholder only pays part of the bill, he or she must pay interest to the bank on the amount of money that is still owing. Some cards require the cardholder to pay the total amount each month.

How can I get a credit card?

When you apply to a bank for a credit card, you must sign an agreement with the bank saying that you will repay all the money charged on your credit card, plus interest. Before a bank will give you a card you must have a good credit history. If you have no credit history, or the credit card company or bank is not sure of your ability to repay the charges on your card, someone may have to cosign your agreement with the bank. Sometimes the bank may require you to keep a cash deposit, or savings account, in the bank as collateral against the line of credit on your credit account.

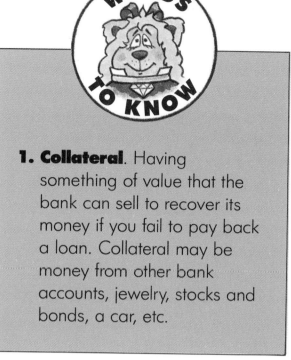

What is the difference between a credit card and a check?

When a person uses a credit card he or she is really taking a loan from the bank. The bank pays the store and then bills the customer for the money he or she charged on the credit card. When a customer pays by check, he or she has to have money in the bank. The check is an order to the bank to pay the store some of that money.

Must I always pay interest if I use a credit card?

It depends on your agreement with the bank. Some banks charge no interest if you pay the full amount on your credit card bill each month, but you usually pay an annual fee. Others charge interest from the day you make a charge. Some credit card companies require you to pay the full amount you owe at the end of the month. Others let you pay part of the amount of money you owe—just like an installment loan—and charge interest on the balance.

How do places that accept bank credit cards get paid?

The banks and other financial institutions pay the stores for everything that is charged on the card. The bank charges the stores a small percentage for this service.

MONEY EVERYWHERE

HOW DOES THE ECONOMY WORK?

WHAT IS THE FOREIGN EXCHANGE MARKET?

HOW MUCH MONEY DOES THE FEDERAL GOVERNMENT OWE?

WHAT IS INFLATION?

WHAT MAKES THE DOLLAR WEAK OR STRONG?

How does the economy work?

All governments try to have high employment with economic growth and minimum price increases. Countries try to control the amount of money that is in circulation because the quantity of money affects how much the economy grows, the level of employment, and the prices of everything that people need. When the money supply increases, or when people can easily borrow money, they spend more and their demand for products increases. As their demand increases, manufacturers need to produce more, which leads to hiring more workers. When there are more workers there is then more money spent in the economy which leads to further economic growth.

If manufacturers can't increase their output, prices rise. A continuing rise in prices is called *inflation*. If wages don't increase to keep up with prices, then people have less to spend. When people have less money to spend, products remain unsold and manufacturers reduce production. This leads to a cutback in workers and unemployment. Thus all governments need to control their money supply.

How much money does the Federal Government owe?

The Federal Government owes more than a trillion dollars. If this debt was divided among every man, woman, and child in the United States, each person would owe about $8,000.

Capitol Building in Washington, D.C.

What is the origin of the United States national debt?

In 1790 Congress assumed $75 million in debts which the individual states had accumulated during the Revolutionary War. National debt was part of the deliberate policy of the first secretary of the Treasury, Alexander Hamilton, who wished to establish a federal debt in order to provide a reason for establishing a federal tax system.

The War of 1812 caused the national debt to grow to $128 million, an amount that was repaid over the next two decades. By 1866, however, the U.S. had incurred a new debt of $2.8 billion because of the Civil War. This amount was not yet fully repaid when the United States entered World War I. This was the beginning of huge increases in the national debt which have continued ever since.

How does the United States Government borrow the money it needs?

When the government has to borrow money, it sells treasury bills and notes, treasury bonds, and savings bonds. These are bought by American and foreign private individuals and financial institutions, and by foreign governments. The United States Government promises to pay the owner the value of each bond plus interest at a future date. Most of our national debt is owed to Americans.

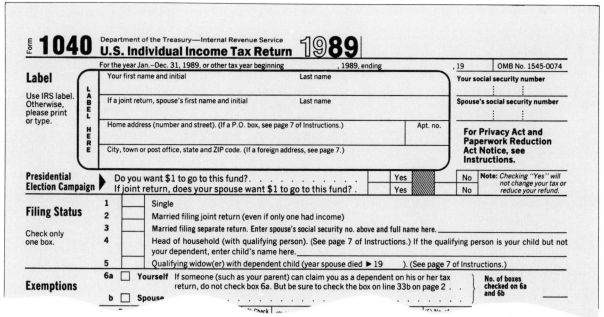

Federal tax form

91

What is the Fed?

The Fed is the Federal Reserve System, the central bank of the United States. The system is the government's bank. It is divided into twelve regional banks that are spread across the country. The Fed's main work is to control the supply of money. It holds a percentage of the funds—the reserves—of commercial banks, and lends money to them when they really need it.

The Fed was created in 1913 by Congress to stabilize the nation's economy. It does this in several ways:

1. It controls the flow of money.

2. It regulates and supervises banking.

3. It administers federal consumer credit protection laws.

4. It makes sure that there is enough coin and paper money to meet public demand.

5. It handles the government's checking accounts.

6. It buys and sells dollars on the international money markets.

7. It processes the millions of checks that are passed between banks every day.

8. The Federal Reserve Bank in New York is the storehouse for about 11,000 tons of gold.

What else does the Federal Reserve do?

The Federal Reserve is the watchdog of the banking industry. Officials from the Fed regularly check banks' records to make sure they are following banking regulations.

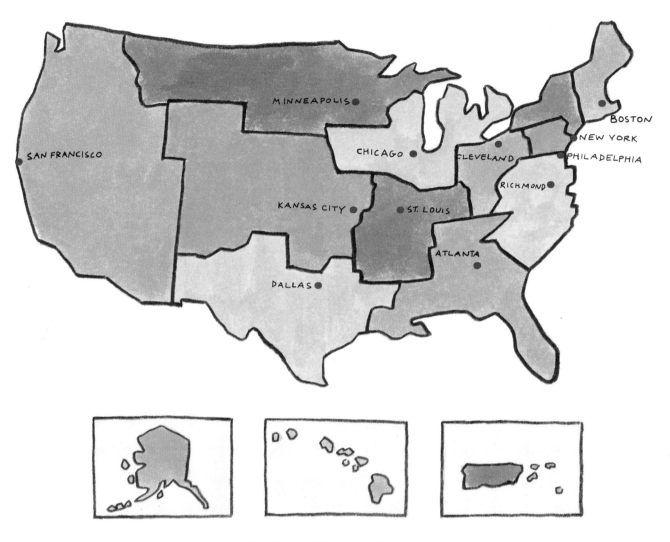

The Federal Reserve Banks

How does the Federal Reserve regulate money?

The Fed is like a traffic cop for money. When the Fed sees there is too much traffic—money—in the economy, it slows down the traffic. It does this by requiring banks to put more money in reserve. When that happens banks charge their customers more interest on loans. The more banks charge, the less people can borrow.

When there is not enough money in the economy the Fed allows the banks to keep less money in reserve. The banks can then lower the interest rate and lend more money to their customers. That way more money comes into the economy.

What is inflation?

Inflation is a word we hear often these days. It means that anything you buy—a good or a service—costs more than it used to. It means that prices have increased or "inflated."

Most experts agree that inflation is due to big increases in the money supply. These increases give people more money to spend on goods and services. When factories are operating as fast as they can and producing goods, it is difficult to meet the increased demand. The result is that prices are forced up as too much money is trying to buy too few goods.

If the economy of a country is balanced, then there is no inflation. Goods and services cost the same amount from year to year. When there is inflation the cost of goods and services goes up, and the value of money goes down. During an inflationary period prices increase because demand exceeds the amount of goods available.

WATCH THESE BALLOONS RISE AS I INFLATE THEM!

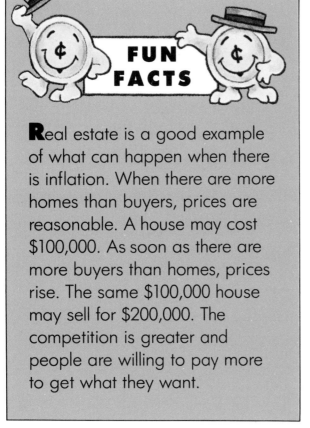

FUN FACTS

Real estate is a good example of what can happen when there is inflation. When there are more homes than buyers, prices are reasonable. A house may cost $100,000. As soon as there are more buyers than homes, prices rise. The same $100,000 house may sell for $200,000. The competition is greater and people are willing to pay more to get what they want.

What happens to the value of money when there is inflation?

It goes down. What you buy for a dollar today will cost you two dollars tomorrow. This means your money is worth less than it was before inflation because it takes twice as much money to buy the same things.

What is a recession?

A recession is a "downturn" in the economy. When sales of goods begin to drop, factories have less orders, and money is "tighter" in the economy. A recession is not as serious as a depression.

How much did people earn in 1900 and what do they earn now?

In 1900 the average hourly wage was 22 cents an hour. In 1990 the average hourly wage was $7.45 an hour. In 1900 the average person worked 59 hours a week making a total of $12.98 a week. In 1990 the average person worked 40 hours a week making a total of $306.80 a week.

What is a depression?

A depression is an economic condition marked by large numbers of people out of work and a big decrease in business. If inflation is a condition in which there are too few goods and too much money, a depression is characterized by having too many goods and too little money. During a depression, not enough people can afford to buy goods that are on the market. As a result, factories stop producing and shut down and many people lose their jobs. When people lose their jobs, they have less money to spend. Then more goods are unsold and more factories close and more workers are laid off.

What happens to the value of money in a depression?

The value of money increases. When there are too many goods for sale people will sell them for less money rather than not sell them at all. Something that costs a dollar in normal times may only cost fifty cents in a depression. Also, people are willing to work for less money—just to have a job, so production costs are lower.

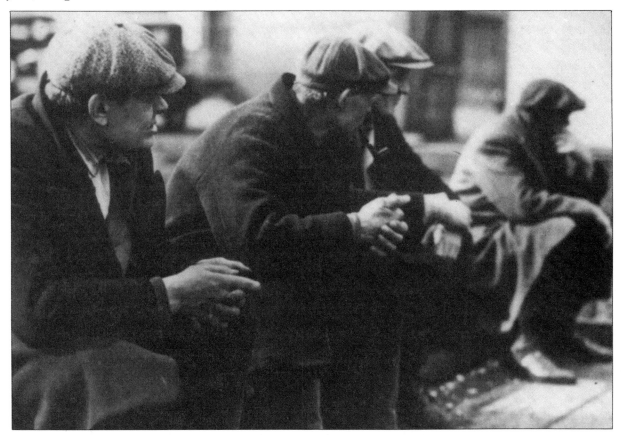

Unemployed men during the Great Depression

96

What was the Great Depression?

The Great Depression occurred in 1929 and lasted for ten years. It was world wide. In the United States almost one third of the workers had no jobs. As people lost their jobs and faith in the economy they withdrew their money from the banks. When so many people demanded their money the banks couldn't meet their demands. The banks had to close their doors and declare bankruptcy. Millions of people lost their homes and their savings when the banks collapsed. During the first three years of the Great Depression almost 10,000 banks closed.

FUN FACTS

Because so many people lost their life's savings when the banks failed in the Depression, Congress created the Federal Deposit Insurance Corporation (FDIC) to protect deposits.

Now anyone who puts money into a bank that is insured by the FDIC has their bank account insured for up to $100,000. If the bank fails, the FDIC will pay the depositors.

How did the United States economy recover from the Great Depression?

During the Depression, the majority of the American people looked to the federal government for help. Measures were taken by President Herbert Hoover and President Franklin Roosevelt to restore faith in the economy and to provide relief for unemployed workers. Under Roosevelt's New Deal, the government established the Public Works Administration which created new jobs and a greater demand for materials. As factories employed more people to meet this demand, incomes increased and the demand for consumer goods rose as well. However, these programs were not enough to end depression conditions. The economy did not fully recover until the United States' involvement in World War II created a demand for workers and stimulated industry and agriculture.

What is foreign exchange?

In the United States the currency is the dollar. If everyone in the world used dollars, life would be simple. But every country has its own money. Just as there were problems when people bartered, so it is today with different currencies. In France the currency is the franc, in Germany it is the mark, in Japan the yen, in India the rupee. When you visit a foreign country, you have to exchange your dollars for the currency of that country. When a country buys products, it usually has to pay for them in the currency of the country it is buying from, so money has to be exchanged. The value of one country's money against another's is called foreign exchange.

What is the foreign exchange market?

The foreign exchange market is the place where foreign exchange dealers in major cities like New York, London, Tokyo, and Paris trade money of different countries. The exchange rate is based on supply and demand and expresses the buying power of one nation's money in relation to another's.

For instance, if Americans buy Japanese goods, they need Japanese yen to pay for the goods. This creates a demand for the yen and so the value of the yen goes up. When the value of the yen goes up, Japanese goods become more expensive. If the goods become too expensive, people will buy less Japanese goods, so then the value of the yen will fall. Often to stop the value of their currency from falling, governments will buy their own currency in the foreign exchange market. Or if the price is too high, governments will sell currency to bring the price down. The value of currencies changes slightly each day.

FUN FACTS

In 1926 a first-class postage stamp cost 2¢. Most bus fares were 10¢. A pound of steak cost 37¢.

In 1936 a pair of men's boxer shorts cost 75¢. A pound of butter cost 37¢. Dinner at a hotel in New York cost $1.75.

In 1946 a quart of milk cost 15¢. A pound of sugar cost 7¢. A pound of coffee cost 40¢.

What makes the dollar weak or strong?

Three things: the amount of inflation, the amount of foreign investment, and the amount of foreign trade. (Goods we sell outside of the United States are exports; goods we buy from other countries are imports.)

When inflation is high and foreign investors can earn high interest they invest in the United States. This makes the dollar strong. When interest is low, then there is less foreign investment and so the dollar weakens.

Every time you buy something that is not made in the United States, you are sending money out of the country and not supporting the American dollar. When you buy products that are made in the United States, your money stays in America and supports American industry. When the profits stay in America, the manufacturers can expand their factories and so employ more people.

WHAT IS A STOCK?

WHY DO COMPANIES
SELL STOCK?

THE STOCK
MARKET

WHAT IS A
BULL MARKET?

WHAT IS A BOND?

WHAT IS THE
DIFFERENCE BETWEEN
STOCKS AND BONDS?

What is the stock market?

The stock market is like a supermarket for buying or selling shares in different companies. If there are many people who want to buy a share in a company, the price of the shares will go up. If there are many people who want to sell shares in a company, the price of the shares will go down.

What is a stock?

Stocks are shares in a company. Stocks are like bricks in a building. If you can't afford to own the whole building, you can buy a few bricks in the building. That gives you a share in the building. Owning stock means that you are a part owner (stockholder) of the company. So you own a share of everything the company owns. When the company makes a profit, the value of your shares goes up. If the company makes a loss the value of your shares goes down. The shares can go down so far that you lose the money you invested in the company.

What is a stockbroker?

A stockbroker is a person who buys and sells shares for other people on the stock market. Stockbrokers must obey rules and regulations so that people who buy stock through them are protected against dishonesty.

What is a stockholder?

A stockholder is a person who holds stock (shares) in a company.

Why do companies sell stock?

It's a way to raise money without going into debt. The owners of the company decide to "go public." This means they sell shares in their company to whoever wants to buy the shares. The money from the shares brings money into the company, and the company can expand and grow or develop new products. The owners decide how many shares they will sell to the public. It can be 100, 1,000, 100,000, or more. Anyone can buy shares in a public company.

Why do people buy stock?

People buy stock to earn money. They think the company will grow and be profitable. There are two ways people who buy stock can make money. They can receive a share of profits, or they can sell the stock if its value increases.

WORDS TO KNOW

1. Dividend. A share of the profits received by a stockholder.

THE MORE RISK... THE MORE RETURN!

What is a proxy?

Every year shareholders are invited to the annual shareholders' meeting. At the meeting they may vote on certain future company plans. Every share is worth one vote, so the more shares a person has, the more power he or she has.

A few weeks before the annual shareholders' meeting, companies send shareholders a voting card so that if they do not plan to come to the shareholders' meeting they can still vote by mailing in the card. This card is called a *proxy*.

What do the terms *bull market* and *bear market* mean?

In the stock market a bull market means stock prices are rising, and a bear market means that the prices of stocks are falling.

What is the stock market report?

Every day the results of trading — the buying and selling of stock and the prices that stocks were bought and sold for — are reported. This is the stock market report.

What is a bond?

A bond is a loan to a government, a government agency, or a large company. When governments want to raise money to build roads or bridges or large companies want to build new factories, they issue bonds. As with most loans, the agency or company taking the loan must pay interest to the bond holder. It is usually for a fixed time and has a fixed interest rate. The bond holder receives regular interest payments. Bond owners often sell their bonds before their maturity date.

How do you make money when you buy or sell a bond?

Like most loans a bond has a fixed rate of interest for a fixed time. If the bond interest is set at 12% and interest rates go down, the bond becomes more valuable because it is earning interest at more than the market rate. If the interest rates go up, the bond becomes less valuable because it is earning interest at less than the market rate.

What is the difference between stocks and bonds?

Only corporations can issue stock. Governments and corporations can issue bonds. When you buy stock you are buying a share in a company. When you buy bonds, you are lending money to the government agency or company issuing the bond. A bond holder usually receives fixed interest payments regularly and the full price of the bond at maturity.

New York Stock Exchange

FUN FACTS

When a company decides to sell stock it is called "floating an issue."

Any stock that sells for less than a dollar is called a penny stock.

Why are blue chip stocks called blue chip?

In poker the most valuable chips in the game are always blue. So blue chip has also come to mean valuable stocks that have very little chance of losing money.

LOOK, BUCK...
I GOT A
BLUE CHIP!

Which is better for my savings: a stock, a bond, or a savings account?

Whenever you are saving or investing your money you have to look at something called *risk/return trade-off*. This means the safer you want your investment to be, the less money you will earn on your investment. The riskier your investment, the more money you can earn, but the riskier it is, the more chance that you could lose your investment.

If you got the same interest rate for your money whether you invested it in a government savings bond or stock in a company, you would choose the government bond. The government is going to be here for a long time, but the company could go bankrupt. Therefore, the company has to offer you a higher return on your money so that you will invest in it. You have to be willing to risk losing your money in the hope of making more money. So, if you want to be sure the money is there when you need it, don't gamble with it. Put it in a government bond. But if you have some money to spare—money you can afford to lose—then you can invest it in something riskier.

HOW DO YOU START A
BUSINESS?

WHAT IS A MARKET
SURVEY?

YOUR OWN
MONEY

HOW DO YOU MAKE A
BUDGET?

WHY DO PEOPLE HAVE
TO PAY TAXES?

WHAT IS A CHARITY?

Starting your own business:

Most people in America work for someone or a company, but many people have their own business. Starting a business is hard work. It takes creativity, organizational skills, and courage. It means taking a chance—but if it is successful it can be very rewarding. Some people are content with a small business, but a small business can grow into a multimillion-dollar company.

What types of businesses are there?

There are two basic types of businesses. A manufacturing business, where something is made and sold, and a service business, where some sort of service—such as dry cleaning or mowing lawns—is provided for money or a fee.

How do you start a business?

First you need to know what kind of business you want. But before you start, you need to find out if your business has a chance of succeeding.

FUN FACTS

If you were offered a job that paid a penny the first day, 2¢ the second day, 4¢ the third day, and continued to double every day, should you take it? Definitely. After 31 days you will have earned $21,474,836.

How do you do that?

One way to start is to conduct a market survey.

What is a market survey?

A market survey asks people questions about their likes and dislikes. It also asks what services or products they would use, and how much they would be willing to pay for them. Their answers help businesspeople decide what products or services have a good chance of succeeding.

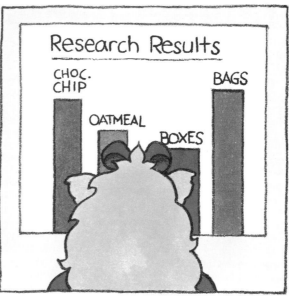

What else do I need?

You need a business plan.

What is a business plan?

It is a plan of what your business will be like and where it will be. It tells what will be sold, and how it will be sold. It tells who the customers will be, how much it will cost to start the business, how much it will cost to run the business, and what the profits are expected to be. It also tells where you will get the money to start your business. To work out the financial needs of your business you need to make a budget.

Can anyone start a business?

Anyone can start his or her own business, but usually first that person has to get legal documents, such as a business license and registration. Even people who sell umbrellas or newspapers on the sidewalk need a license. If you sell food, you usually need a health certificate or approval from a government health organization.

How do you make a budget?

Suppose you are going to start a business making and selling cookies. First you need to know how many cookies you can sell each month, and how much it will cost to make the cookies. This will include the cost of the ingredients, rent, electricity, and gas, as well as wages if you need to pay someone to help you make the cookies. You have to add to this the cost of marketing and selling the cookies. These costs include advertising, bags for the cookies you sell, and a place from which to sell them. To all of these costs you must add your start-up costs. (These are one-time costs and might include baking tins and utensils and a stove.)

What does *Inc.* mean?

Inc. is short for *incorporated*. When a company has *Inc.* after its name, it means that the company is incorporated. There are special business laws for incorporated businesses.

Most people who open a small business are responsible for all the business debts. If the business fails, they often have to sell everything they own to pay their debts. But if the business is incorporated, the responsibility for the debts is limited to the value of the business only.

What happens after you start a business?

After you have been selling your cookies for a while, you need to see if you are making a profit or a loss. If your expenses for producing and selling the cookies are more than the money the business has taken in, then you will have made a loss. If you have money left over after you have paid all the business expenses, then you will have made a profit. If you make a profit in business, you will have to pay taxes.

Why do people have to pay taxes?

Tax is the money the government collects from people and businesses when they earn money or make a profit. Taxes go to pay for all the services the government provides as well as for schools, libraries, some hospitals, roads and bridges, and for the armed forces.

Why do we have different kinds of taxes?

Cities, states, and the federal government all need to raise money, so they all levy taxes on companies and people who earn money.

What happens if I don't pay my taxes?

It is illegal and you can be sent to jail.

FUN FACTS

In 1988 the IRS estimated that 43% of the people who paid federal income tax paid too little. This underpayment cost the government $64 billion.

In 1989 the total amount of income tax collected by the federal government was $424.2 billion.

When did people first have to pay taxes?

Taxation is ancient. Even thousands of years ago people had to pay part of their earnings to their government. Archaeologists have found that in ancient Egypt taxes were paid with a share of the crops produced on private lands, or by forced labor on public lands.

How does the government decide how much tax people should pay?

The government looks at two things when it sets tax levels: how much money it needs and how much people can pay. The government makes a budget to know how much money it will spend to run the country and then decides how much of this money can be collected in taxes. How much a person must pay is decided by how much they earn and how many people they must support. People who earn more money usually have to pay more taxes than those who earn less.

FUN FACTS

During the reign of Louis XIV of France, in the 17th century, more than half of the tax money collected was spent just collecting the taxes. The cost of collecting taxes in the United States today is 1% of the money collected.

How can you earn money without starting a "real" business?

There are lots of ways that young people can earn money without actually opening a business. Two of the most popular ways to earn money are baby-sitting and mowing lawns. But there are dozens of other ways. If you are a good student you can coach other students, or help younger students with their homework. You can help to look after someone's pet, or look after their plants, while they are away. All it takes is some creative thinking, which is exactly what is needed to start a "real" business.

What is a budget?

A budget is a plan that will tell you how much money you have, and how to plan ahead so that you have money for the things you need. It is a way to get a clear picture of what you are spending your money on.

To know where your money goes, keep a written record of all your spending for a few weeks. You will soon learn where you can cut down on your spending and save money. Then you can set up a budget. The questions to ask yourself when you set up a budget are:

How much do I have from my allowance, gifts, jobs?

What have I bought?
How much do I have left?
How much can I save?

Before you buy anything, ask yourself:

What do I want to buy?
How much does it cost?
How much have I saved so far?
How much more do I need?

Before you borrow money, ask yourself:

How much do I need to borrow?
How much can I pay back at a time?
Can I save my own money, so I
don't need to borrow?

Managing money can be very simple once you understand that what you have to spend is *all* you have to spend. Remember, when you borrow money, you have to pay back the money you borrow plus a little extra (interest). Always think carefully before borrowing money.

What is a charity?

Giving to someone who is less fortunate than you or sending money to an appeal is a charity.

Why should I give to charity?

It is your responsibility as a citizen of the world to give help to people who are less fortunate than you. No matter how little you have, you should help other people. You can do this in lots of different ways. You can give away your old toys and your clothes you have outgrown. You can read to someone who is blind or you can give money to someone who is not as lucky as you.

Where does your money go?

This is one of the most important questions you have to ask once you have money of your own to spend and save and use to make more money. Keeping track of how much you have, what you are spending it on, and knowing whether or not you can afford to buy what you want are the secrets to success with money. Having a budget helps.

A FINAL WORD ABOUT MONEY

Many people say that money is the root of all evil. And it is true that some people are so greedy or so desperate for money that they will rob or even kill for it. But much good can be done with money, and many people use their money to help others less fortunate than themselves. Organizations such as UNICEF, Save the Children, and many others rely on the generosity of ordinary people for their money. Most universities have funds for scholarships to help poor students or to fund research. Many hospitals and homes for old people or children are funded by charities. Museums and concert halls are also funded by donations. In fact there is hardly an artistic organization that does not receive financial help from generous people.

Every single day of your life you are dealing with money. Understanding money is a life skill. Understanding about money, how to use it, and not abuse it, is very important. It can make your life enjoyable, fun, comfortable, productive, and rewarding or it can be disastrous. It can ruin your life, and if you abuse it you can go to jail. Money can be the best thing and the most positive, or the worst thing. It's up to you. You have to take responsibility for yourself and for your money, to understand it and enjoy it. You have to live within the money you have, you have to budget your money, and plan for the future.

The Buck Stops Here!

GLOSSARY

account Money deposited in a bank which may be withdrawn on demand by the depositor

Automated Teller Machine (ATM) A machine in a bank or at some other convenient place where people can withdraw or deposit money electronically

bank An institution where money may be safely kept and which lends money and provides other financial services

bank note Previously, a note issued by a bank and used in place of money, it entitled the owner to payment on demand at the bank. Today, paper money (bank notes) is issued by the Federal Reserve

bank statement A record of deposits, withdrawals, fees charged, and interest earned on a particular account

bargaining A discussion between a seller and a buyer about the value of a good or service

barter To trade a good or a service with someone for a different good or service without using money

blue chip The highest valued chip in a poker game, and also the name of the best stocks on the stock market

bond A certificate issued by a company or government agency that needs to borrow money

budget A plan of how much money a person, business, government, or another organization has to spend and how it will be spent

Bureau of Engraving and Printing The agency of the United States Government responsible for printing paper money and United States Postal stamps

Certificate of Deposit (CD) A type of savings account where the money is deposited for an agreed amount of time

check A written order to a bank to pay a specified amount of money to a specified person or company, from money on deposit with the bank

check stubs The portion of a check on which you may keep a record of the checks you write

collateral Property which a borrower promises to pay a lender in case of default on a loan

corporation An incorporated business, a business organized so that business responsibilities and liabilities are not those of the people who own the business

cosign To sign a document for another person indicating responsibility if the borrower defaults

counterfeit To make a copy of something which people will think is real

credit Money loaned, usually for a fee, which may be paid back at a future time

credit card A card which allows people to make purchases on credit

credit check The record of a person's credit history which lending institutions use to determine whether or not that person is financially reliable

currency Any kind of money that is used as a medium of exchange

debt The money you owe when you buy on credit or borrow from someone else

default To fail to pay back a loan

denomination A category of bills of particular value

deposit To place in a bank. Also the sum of money which is put there

depression A period of serious recession marked by high unemployment and a decline in business and stock market values

dividends The profits which a company distributes to its stockholders

economic growth   An economic condition marked by high employment and an increasing demand for, and production of, goods and services

economy   The structure of the flow of money in a society

electrum   A natural mixture of gold and silver

Federal Reserve   The central bank of the United States

fee   A fixed charge

foreign exchange   The value of one nation's currency against another's

foreign exchange market   The place where foreign exchange dealers in major cities around the world trade the money of different countries

Fort Knox   An army base in Kentucky where most of the United States' gold is stored

good   Anything of some value which may be traded for or bought

hedge against inflation   An investment made now to protect a person or business from the risk of rising or falling prices in the future

Inc.   abbreviation for "incorporated"

incorporation   A business which has formed a corporation and thereby limited its liability

Individual Retirement Account (IRA)   A tax deferred account used to save money for retirement

inflation   An economic condition characterized by rising prices, it is usually caused by too much available money in the economy

installment credit   An arrangement between a store and a consumer which allows a purchase to be paid for in partial payments

installment   Partial payment of a debt

invest   To risk money with hope of added financial return

Keogh Account   A tax deferred retirement savings account for a person who is self-employed

line of credit   An agreed amount of money waiting at the bank to be borrowed by a depositor

loan   A sum of money borrowed for a certain period of time, often involving interest paid to the lender by the borrower

market survey   A survey conducted by a business to find out what people will want to buy

maturity The end of a bond's interest-earning term or the last day when a financial instrument is due

medium of exchange   Anything that a group of people agree has a certain value

milled coin   A coin with ridged edges

mint   To make coins out of metal, or the place where coins are made

money   Anything a group of people accept in exchange for goods or services

Money Market Account   A savings account with relatively low interest which allows you to write a limited number of checks

money order   An order issued from a post office or a bank to pay a specified sum of money to a specified person or business, it may be cashed at any post office or bank

mortgage money   Money loaned by a bank for the purpose of buying a house or other property

obela   An early Greek coin noted for its extremely small size

Passbook Account   A savings account in which the transactions are recorded in a book which must be given to the bank whenever a deposit or withdrawal is made

penny stock   Shares of stock that cost less than a dollar each

Personal Identification Number (PIN) The secret number encoded onto a bank card which must be entered into the ATM before money can be withdrawn or deposited

piece of eight Spanish dollar used in the American colonies and the early United States as a medium of exchange

PIN Personal Identification Number used with a money machine card

prime rate The interest rate that banks charge their largest and best customers

profit The money a business makes less the costs of producing and selling its products

proxy A voting card mailed in by a shareholder who does not attend the annual shareholders' meeting

pygg A type of clay which was used to make the jars in which people stored money, the word is the origin of our modern day "piggy bank"

quarter eagle United States gold $2.50 coin issued in 1796

real estate Property in land and buildings

recession A "downturn" in the economy, when the demand for goods declines and the money supply is less

register The section of a checkbook where you may record your transactions

risk/return trade-off The relationship between an investment's risk and its potential for making money

savings Money that is put somewhere safe so that it can be used later

secretary of the Treasury Presidential appointee who directs the Department of the Treasury and advises the President in financial matters

service Any work that can be done for money or barter

share A part of a company which may be bought by someone as an investment

stock   Shares of a company which may be purchased by the public

stock market   Place where shares of many different companies are bought and sold

stockbroker   A person who buys and sells shares for other people on the stock market

stockholder   A person who owns stock (shares) in a company

Treasury, Department of the   The executive department of the U.S. Government which is responsible for the management of federal funds, including the coinage and printing of money

unemployment   The rate of people in a society who want to work but are unable to find jobs

value   The worth of something as measured in goods, services, or a medium of exchange

The Children's Financial Network

The Children's Financial Network was founded by Neale S. Godfrey. Its aim is to teach children about money, its uses and purpose. It does this via various learning programs, books, and toys. Under the umbrella of the Children's Financial Network programs, children learn to budget their money, have their own savings accounts and savings cards, their own insurance policies, and stocks. By educating children in this way, the Children's Financial Network hopes to put an end to the abysmal financial illiteracy that afflicts most Americans. If children learn to understand money when they are young, they will grow up to be financially responsible and solvent adults.

Neale S. Godfrey was born in New York City and raised in West Caldwell, New Jersey. She got her start as an entrepreneur at the age of ten when she posted signs on the local storm sewers and charged the neighborhood kids 25¢ each for a "tour of the sewer."

After graduating from The American University in Washington, D.C., Neale worked at The Chase Manhattan Bank, where she enjoyed a successful thirteen-year career. In 1985 she left Chase to become president of The First Women's Bank. She built its $50,000,000 in assets to $600,000,000 in three and a half years.

While at The First Women's Bank, Neale pursued an interest she had been working on for years: finance for children. She opened The First Children's Bank (Division of The First Women's Bank, now First New York Bank For Business) at FAO Schwarz in New York in 1988.